Golightly Educational Center
5536 St. Antoine
Detroit, Michigan 48202

To Julie and Steve —
with thanks and love

Adventures in Storytelling

The Girl from the Sky
An Inca Folktale from South America

Retold by Anamarie Garcia

Illustrated by Janice Skivington

CHILDRENS PRESS ®
CHICAGO

Adventures in Storytelling

Dear Parents and Teachers,

Adventures in Storytelling Books have been designed to delight storytellers of all ages and to make world literature available to nonreaders as well as to those who speak English as a second language. The wordless format and accompanying audiocassette make it possible for both readers and nonreaders who are unacquainted with a specific ethnic folktale to use either the visual or the audio portion as an aid in understanding the story.

For additional reference the complete story text is printed in the back of the book, and post-story activities are suggested for those who enjoy more participation.

The history of storytelling

"Once upon a time . . . ."

"Long ago but not so long ago that we cannot remember . . . ."

"In the grey, grey beginnings of the world . . . ."

"And it came to pass, more years ago than I can tell you . . . ."

These are magic words. They open kingdoms and countries beyond our personal experiences and make the impossible possible and the miraculous, if not commonplace, at least not unexpected.

For hundreds of years people have been telling stories. You do it every day, every time you say, "You'll never believe what happened to me yesterday"; or "You know, something like that happened to my grandmother, but according to her, it went something like this . . . ."

Before video recorders, tape recorders, television, and radio, there was storytelling. It was the vehicle through which every culture remembered its past and kept alive its heritage. It was the way people explained life, shared events, and entertained themselves around the fire on dark, lonely nights. The stories they told evoked awe and respect for tradition, ritual, wisdom, and power; transmitted cultural taboos and teachings from generation to generation; and made people laugh at the foolishness in life or cry when confronted by life's tragedies.

As every culture had its stories, so too did each have its storytellers. In Africa they were called griots; in Ireland, seanachies; in France, troubadours; and in the majority of small towns and villages around the world they were simply known as the gifted. Often their stories were hundreds of years old. Some of them were told exactly as they had been told for centuries; others were changed often to reflect people's interests and where and how they lived.

With the coming of the printing press and the availability of printed texts, the traditional storyteller began to disappear — not altogether and not everywhere, however. There were pockets in the world where stories were kept alive by those who remembered them and believed in them. Although not traditional storytellers, these people continued to pass down folktales, even though the need for formal, professional storytelling was fading.

In the nineteenth century, the Grimm brothers made the folktale fashionable, and for the first time collections of tales from many countries became popular. Story collections by Andrew Lang, Joseph Jacobs, and Charles Perrault became the rage, with one important difference: these stories were written down to be read, not told aloud to be heard.

As the nineteenth century gave way to the twentieth, there was a revival of interest in storytelling. Spearheaded by children's librarians and schoolteachers, a new kind of storytelling evolved — one that was aimed specifically at children and connected to literature and reading. The form of literature most chosen by these librarians and teachers was the traditional folktale.

During this time prominent educator May Hill Arbuthnot wrote that children were a natural audience for folktales because the qualities found in these tales were those to which children normally responded in stories: brisk action, humor, and an appeal to a sense of justice. Later, folklorist Max Luthi supported this theory. He called the folktale a fundamental building block, an outstanding aid in child development, and the archetypal form of literature that lays the groundwork for all literature.

By the middle of the twentieth century, storytelling was seen as a way of exposing children to literature that they would not discover by themselves and of making written language accessible to those who could not read it by themselves. Storytelling became a method of promoting an understanding of other cultures and a means of strengthening the cultural awareness of the listening group; a way of creating that community of listeners that evolves when a diverse group listens to a tale well-told.

Many of these same reasons for storytelling are valid today — perhaps even more relevant than they were nearly one hundred years ago. Current research confirms what librarians and teachers have known all along — that storytelling provides a practical, effective, and enjoyable way to introduce children to literature while fostering a love of reading. It connects the child to the story and the book. Through storytelling, great literature (the classics, poetry, traditional folktales) comes alive; children learn to love language and experience the beauty of the spoken word, often before they master those words by reading them themselves.

Without exception, all cultures have accumulated a body of folktales that represent their history, beliefs, and language. Yet, while each culture's folktales are unique, they also are connected to the folktales of other cultures through the universality of themes contained within them. Some of the most common themes appearing in folktales around the world deal with good overcoming evil; the clever outwitting the strong; and happiness being the reward for kindness to strangers, the elderly, and the less fortunate. We hear these themes repeated in stories from quaint Irish villages along the Atlantic coast to tiny communities spread throughout the African veldt and from cities and towns of the industrialized Americas to the magnificent palaces of the emperors of China and Japan. It is these similarities that are fascinating; that help us to transcend the barriers of language, politics, custom, and religion; and that bind us together as "the folk" in folktales.

Using wordless picture books and audiocassettes

Every child is a natural storyteller. Children begin telling stories almost as soon as they learn to speak. The need to share what they experience and how they perceive life prompts them to organize their thoughts and express themselves in a way others will understand. But storytelling goes beyond the everyday need to communicate. Beyond the useful, storytelling can be developed into a skill that entertains and teaches. Using wordless picture books and audiocassettes aids in this process.

When children hear a story told, they are learning much about language, story structure, plot development, words, and the development of a "sense of story." Wordless books encourage readers to focus on pictures for the story line and the sequence of events, which builds children's visual skills. In time, the "visually literate" child will find it easier to develop verbal and written skills.

Because a wordless folktale book is not restricted by reading ability or educational level, it can be used as a tool in helping children and adults, both English and non-English speakers, as well as readers and nonreaders to understand or retell a story from their own rich, ethnic perspective. Listening to folktales told on an audiocassette or in person offers another advantage; it allows the listener, who may be restricted by reading limitations, to enjoy literature, learn about other cultures, and develop essential prereading skills. Furthermore, it gives them confidence to retell stories on their own and motivates them to learn to read them.

Something special happens when you tell a story; something special happens when you hear a story well-told. Storytelling is a unique, entertaining, and powerful art form, one that creates an intimate bond between storyteller and listener, past and present. To take a story and give it a new voice is an exhilarating experience; to watch someone else take that same story and make it his or her own is another.

Janice M. Del Negro
Children's Services
The Chicago Public Library

The following folktale originated in South America among the Inca Indians. This tale has been told many times and in many different cultures. It is a story about a young boy and girl whose different worlds eventually keep them apart.

Story text

There once was a man who grew the best potatoes in all the land. One morning, when the man went out to hoe the weeds from his field, he discovered that a large number of his potatoes had been stolen.

The next morning, he made the same discovery — and the next morning after that. Finally, he told his son that he must go to the fields when the sun set, and wait for the thieves. "When you discover who they are," he said, "we'll be able to report them to the authorities."

For two nights, the young man fell asleep at dusk — just before the thieves came. On the third night, however, he forced himself to stay awake.

As the sun began to paint a dim blue and yellow glow behind the mountains, he watched in amazement as the stars began to fall toward the potato field. Faster and faster they came until there was a blinding flash!

In the blink of an eye, hundreds of beautiful, young women stood in the field, each holding a small basket. Their faces were as lovely as morning flowers, and their hair shone like silver streams. Each bent down, uprooted several potatoes, and placed them in her basket.

The young man stood transfixed. "How can creatures so beautiful take that which does not belong to them?" he wondered. "I must talk to one of them — I must!"

And so he leaped from where he was hiding and grabbed one of the maidens. She did not attempt to escape. The others, however, rose quickly into the sky like giant sparks and took their position as stars in the heavens.

"So it was you who took my father's potatoes," said the young man, still holding her tightly.

The star girl stood motionless, looking at him with the most beautiful eyes the young man had ever seen.

At the moment her gaze met his, he knew that he must have this heavenly maiden as his wife. "Please, I beg of you, stay with me," he pleaded.

Then the star girl spoke. "I cannot," she said. "I will die if I stay on earth too long. Please, let me go."

But the young man could not bear the thought of her leaving. So he took her to his home and asked his parents to keep her in the house to prevent her from escaping.

His mother took the young woman's dress and gave her earth clothes. The mother tried to cheer the star girl, but as the days passed, the heavenly maiden became sadder and sadder. The young man and his father tried to cheer her also, but to no avail. As the weeks turned into months, her beautiful glow slowly disappeared.

One day, when the young man and his father were in the fields, the mother looked into star girl's sad eyes and could no longer bear her sorrow. She knew that soon star girl's glow would disappear and she would die. So, she gave the star girl her dress and opened the door for her. Immediately, the star girl's glow returned, and she rose into the sky.

When the young man returned home and saw that his beloved maiden had escaped, he became wild with grief. Heartbroken and sobbing, he climbed the highest mountain, hoping the maiden would come to him. But she did not.

As he sat atop the mountain, a giant condor flew by and asked him the reason for his sadness. When the young man told him, the condor said, "Do not weep. It is true that the star girl has fled to the sky kingdom. But because your sorrow is so great and your love so strong, I will take you to her. Climb upon my back."

Into the sky they flew, higher and higher. The journey took more than a year. Finally, tired, hungry, and ragged, they arrived in the sky kingdom. After several days' rest, the condor led the young man to the shores of a huge lake. Upon looking at their reflections in the water, they saw themselves as a hundred years old! But after bathing in the lake, their youth was restored.

The condor said to the boy, "Now go to the opposite shore of the lake. There, you will find the great temple of the sun and moon. A ceremony will take place in this temple, and the maidens of the sky will be part of it. All the maidens will look like your beloved. Stand perfectly still as they pass you. One of the last maidens in line will be yours. When she touches you with her arm, grab her quickly. Don't let go for any reason."

So the boy went to the temple. Just as the condor said, the star maidens passed him in a single line, and his beloved touched him with her arm. When he grabbed her, she said, "Why have you come all this way? I was coming back to you."

The star maiden took the young man to her home, where she hid him. She told him, "If my parents knew you were here, they would send us both away."

For a year, the star girl fed the young man and kept him warm from the cold winds of the sky. But as time passed, he began to miss the mountains and the fields on earth. One day, sensing his sadness, she said to him, "Your place is not here. The time has come for you to go." Then she turned and sadly walked away.

Thinking that he would never see the star girl again, the young man made his way to the lake. There he saw the condor gliding high above the water. When the giant bird saw the young man, he swooped down. As he looked at the young man, who looked old and tired, the condor knew that he must take his friend back to earth. Before they began their year-long journey, they bathed in the waters of the lake, where they became strong and youthful again. Then they set out on their journey.

Upon their return to earth, the young man's parents, who had thought they would never see their son again, cried with joy. The three of them settled down and lived the rest of their lives growing potatoes. The young man never forgot the beautiful star girl who had taken not only part of his father's crops but also all of his heart.

About the storyteller

My name is Anamarie Garcia. I am the storyteller you hear on the tape recording of *The Girl from the Sky*.

I live in Arizona where I am a theatre arts teacher, storyteller, puppeteer, actress, director, and creative drama specialist. My most demanding roles, however, are as mother to my four year-old daughter, Rachel, and wife to my husband, Joe.

When I was just a toddler, I was introduced to the magic of stories and books. Since then I have come to love words and language. For me, reading stories and telling stories are two of the most precious gems in the treasure chest we call "our imagination." Sharing the wonder of stories — past and present — with children of all ages brings me a lot of joy — joy that I would like to pass on to my daughter and the students I teach.

About the illustrator

I thoroughly enjoyed illustrating this book. It brought me back to my childhood and to dreams of flying. You can see by the picture I have drawn of myself that these dreams are still alive. Through the power of imagination and the magic of the characters I have created, I am able to fly — assisted by a giant condor or as free as the girl from the sky.

It is my hope that others will feel the same freedom of flight that I felt while illustrating this book and experience the joy of learning about another culture.

Project Editor: Alice Flanagan
Design and Electronic Page Composition: Biner Design
Engraver: Liberty Photoengravers
Printer: Lake Book Manufacturing, Inc.

Storytelling activities

Storytelling provides a wonderful opportunity to share information, feelings, and a love of books with children. Through listening, discussion, and a wide variety of post-story activities, children can be helped to understand new ideas, learn and use new words, practice listening skills, experience life outside the dominant culture, and develop writing and storytelling skills. Some of the following activities may be helpful in making this possible:

- Discuss the story. This will give children the opportunity to ask questions and share information they have learned.

- Ask children to retell the story. This will help you measure their comprehension and interact with them through quiet conversation.

- Ask children to act out the story. Provide generic props (scarves, crowns, masks) and puppets.

- Have paper and magic markers or crayons available so children can draw the story. You might ask them to draw a picture of one of the characters in the book or make a story map (a series of drawings reflecting the sequence of story events).

- Ask children to make cutouts of the story characters and back them with felt or flannel for use on a felt/flannel board. As you retell the story, place the cutouts on the felt/flannel board; then ask the children to retell the story several times. Afterward, comment on their personal variations.

- Help the children write a letter to a favorite story character; or have them pretend to be one of the characters in the story and write a letter to you.

- Ask the children to tell the story from different points of view, each time basing it on the viewpoint of a different character.

- Play the "what if" game. Ask children to tell how the story would be different if the ending changed; if the story took place today instead of "once upon a time"; if the story took place in a different country.

More about storytelling and folktales.

If you'd like to read more about storytelling or other Central and South American folktales, check out some of the following books from your local library:

Pellowski, Anne. *The Family Storytelling Handbook: How to Use Stories, Anecdotes, Rhymes, Handkerchiefs, Paper and Other Objects to Enrich Your Family Traditions.* New York: Macmillan, 1984.

_____. *The Story Vine; A Sourcebook of Unusual and Easy-to-Tell Stories from Around the World.* New York: Macmillan, 1984.

Sierra, Judy and Robert Kaminski. *Multicultural Folktales: Stories to Tell Young Children.* Phoenix: The Oryx Press, 1991.

Sierra, Judy. *Twice Upon a Time: Stories to Tell, Retell, Act Out and Write About.* New York: H. W. Wilson, 1989.

Rohmer, Harriet and Mary Anchondo. *How We Came to the Fifth World.* Emeryville, CA: Children's Book Press, 1987.

Rohmer, Harriet and Dorminster Wilson. *Mother Scorpion Country: A Legend from the Miskito Indians of Nicaragua.* Emeryville, CA: Children's Book Press, 1987.

Library of Congress Cataloging-in-Publication Data
Garcia, Anamarie
    The girl from the sky : an Inca folktale from South America / retold by Anamarie Garcia ; illustrated by Janice Skivington.
       p.   cm.— (Adventures in storytelling)
    Summary: Pictures tell the story of the impossible love between a young potato grower and a star maiden. Text appears at the back of book and suggestions for storytelling activities are given.
     ISBN 0-516-05138-5
    1. Incas — Legends. 2. Storytelling [1. Incas — Legends. 2. Indians of South America — Legends.] I. Skivington, Janice, ill. II. Title. III. Series.

F3429.3.F6G27 1992   91-42163
398.2'098 —dc20   CIP
                                            AC